My Cake

For Christopher

Note: It is not wise to allow children to eat raw cake mix.
The raw ingredients can cause stomach upsets.

For a free color catalog describing Gareth Stevens' list of high-quality books, call 1-800-542-2595 (USA) or 1-800-461-9120 (Canada). Gareth Stevens' Fax: (414) 225-0377.

Library of Congress Cataloging-in-Publication Data

Gore, Sheila.
   My cake / Sheila Gore; photographs by Fiona Pragoff.
      p. cm. — (First step science)
   Includes bibliographical references and index.
   ISBN 0-8368-1186-0
   1. Cake—Juvenile literature. 2. Science—Juvenile literature. [1. Cake. 2. Baking. 3. Science.]
 I. Pragoff, Fiona, ill. II. Title. III. Series.
 TX771.G64 1995
 641.8'653—dc20   94-34039

This edition first published in 1995 by
Gareth Stevens Publishing
1555 North RiverCenter Drive, Suite 201
Milwaukee, Wisconsin 53212, USA

The editor would like to thank Betty Ferris for her kind assistance with the chocolate cake recipe used in this book.

Series editor: Patricia Lantier-Sampon
Editorial assistants: Mary Dykstra, Diane Laska
Illustrations: Alex Ayliffe
Science consultant: Dr. Bryson Gore

Printed in the United States of America
1 2 3 4 5 6 7 8 9 99 98 97 96 95

First Step Science

My Cake

by Sheila Gore
photographs by Fiona Pragoff

Gareth Stevens Publishing
MILWAUKEE

It's my birthday!
All these things
are for my party.

4

I'm going to make my own birthday cake.

This recipe tells me how much
I need of each ingredient.

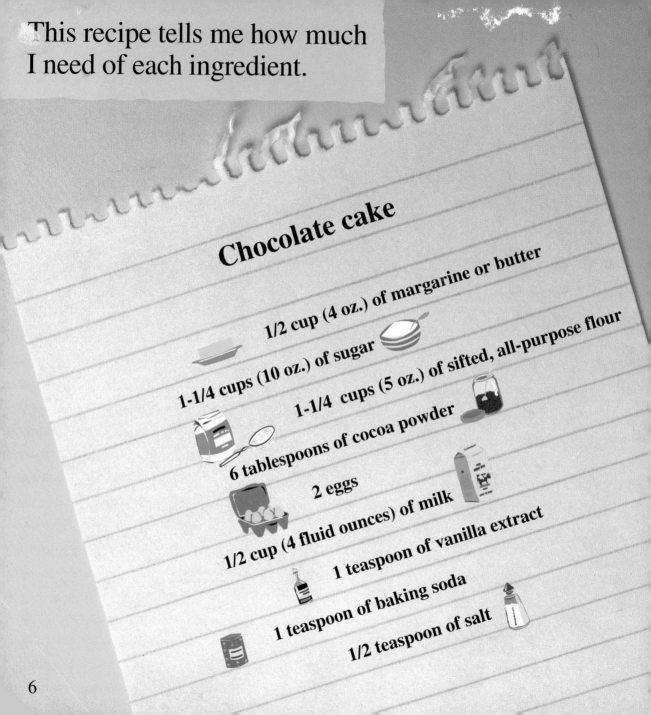

Chocolate cake

1/2 cup (4 oz.) of margarine or butter

1-1/4 cups (10 oz.) of sugar

1-1/4 cups (5 oz.) of sifted, all-purpose flour

6 tablespoons of cocoa powder

2 eggs

1/2 cup (4 fluid ounces) of milk

1 teaspoon of vanilla extract

1 teaspoon of baking soda

1/2 teaspoon of salt

I measure each ingredient carefully.

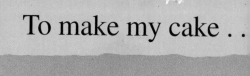

sugar

flour

milk

vanilla extract

need all these ingredients.

margarine

salt

cocoa powder

eggs
2

baking soda

9

Look what happens when I mix
the margarine and the sugar.

Mixing the flour, salt, and baking soda
with the cocoa makes a pale brown powder.

What happens to the eggs when
I whip them and add the milk?

Now I need to blend
all three mixtures.

I pour the egg mixture into the margarine and sugar mixture. Then I add the vanilla extract.

When I add the dry ingredients . . .

how does the mixture change?

15

and puts the pan into a hot oven.

The heat makes my cake rise.

To help my cake
cool down, Dad puts
it on a cooling rack.

18

My cake keeps its shape. It isn't sticky any more.

My cake has tiny holes.

My cake has a hard crust. I can spread icing on top.

I'm decorating
my cake.

22

How old am I?

At my party, there's lots of cake for my friends.

What kind of cake would you like?

25

FOR MORE INFORMATION

Notes for Parents and Teachers

As you share this book with young readers, these notes may help you explain the scientific concepts behind the different activities.

pages 4, 5, 6
Getting ready to bake
It's a good idea to involve the children in shopping for the ingredients. Explain the importance of basic kitchen hygiene, such as washing hands and putting on a clean apron.

pages 6, 7 Measuring things
It is important to weigh exact amounts of each ingredient. If there is too much or too little of anything, the cake will not bake properly.

pages 10, 11, 12, 13, 14, 15
Mixing things
When you mix ingredients in a bowl, the mixing often changes the appearance of the original ingredients. But because the original ingredients can still possibly be separated at this point, this sort of change is reversible. When the cake is baked, however, the ingredients are altered chemically. This change is irreversible because you can no longer separate the original ingredients.

pages 16, 17, 18, 19
Cake pans and cake shapes
Inside the oven, the runny mixture, or batter, sets into a firm cake that is the same shape as the cake pan.

pages 17, 19 Baking cakes

The heat in the oven causes a number of chemical changes to take place:

- The baking soda dissolved in the milk and eggs forms bubbles of gas called carbon dioxide. This also happens with the baking powder in the all-purpose flour. If you managed to beat air into the mixture during the mixing process, there will also be bubbles of air in the mixture. As the mixture gets warmer, the bubbles of air and carbon dioxide grow bigger, which makes the cake rise.
- The bubbles become permanent "holes" when the heat makes the eggs and milk set.
- The flour absorbs moisture from the liquid ingredients and turns into a stiff paste. This paste makes the mixture stiffer and stronger so the walls around the bubbles don't collapse.
- The sugar and margarine hold moisture to make the cake tender.

page 18 Cooling cakes

The cooling rack allows air to circulate around all sides of the cake so it cools faster and does not get soggy.

pages 21, 22 Icing and decorating

The icing used for the cake in this book is a butter cream icing, but almost any icing can be selected.

page 23 Counting candles

The number of candles on a cake provides a good opportunity to practice counting.

pages 24, 25 Sharing the cake

In order to explain fractions, a cake can be divided into portions. This also encourages the idea of sharing.

Things to Do

1. Personalized packaging

Look at a box of packaged cake mix. What ingredients are already included in the mix? What other ingredients need to be added? See what you can learn by reading the nutrition label and other information printed on the box. Then design your own box of cake mix using paper or cardboard and colored markers.

2. Cakes and nutrition

Try changing a favorite cake recipe to make a healthier cake. You can use a little less margarine, replace the sugar with a natural sweetener such as dried fruit or honey, or use oats, bran, or whole wheat flour instead of some of the all-purpose flour. Instead of icing or a cream or jam filling, use a nut cream or paste.

3. Cakes for celebrations

See if you can find out how to make some of the special cakes, such as gingerbread, simnel cake, or rice cakes, that are used in celebrations all over the world.

4. Cupcake yummies

Use the recipe in this book to make cupcakes as well as a regular cake. Guess if it will take your cupcakes a longer or shorter time to bake than the cake. For the cake, you need one 7-inch (18-centimeter)-round baking pan. Grease the pan and dust it with flour or use a nonstick pan. Bake the cake at 350° F (175° C) for 30-35 minutes. Use muffin pans to make the cupcakes. Is there a difference in baking time? Decorate your cake or cupcakes when cool.

Fun Facts about Cakes

1. Margarine was invented by a French chemist about one hundred years ago. It was created to provide an inexpensive fat for soldiers in the French army.

2. When you whip eggs with a whisk or beater, you blend in air. The air expands in the oven and helps baked goods such as cakes and muffins rise.

3. Most of the vanilla in the world comes from Madagascar, an island off the coast of Africa. Vanilla is made from the seedpod of a large orchid.

4. The heaviest cake ever baked weighed over 60 tons. This cake, baked for a special event in Alabama, had over 8 tons of icing alone!

5. The sugar most commonly used in baking is sucrose, which is a natural sugar found in plants such as sugarcane or sugar beets.

6. You can use a toothpick to find out if your cake is finished baking. Stick the toothpick into the middle of the cake. If it comes out clean, without batter sticking to it, the cake is done!

7. Salt is sometimes used in cake recipes to balance and bring out the sweetness of sugar in the recipe.

8. Chocolate and cocoa come from large cacao pods that grow on trees native to South and Central America. Cacao is now also grown in parts of Africa and Asia.

Glossary

baking soda — a special type of salt listed in many recipes.

cake pan — a metal tin or pan used for baking muffins or a cake.

cooling rack — a raised and slotted metal frame or stand used for cooling foods or objects that have been taken out of a hot oven.

crust — the hard outside surface of an object, such as bread or the Earth.

decorating — making a design or pattern.

extract — a concentrated natural flavoring, such as vanilla, banana, or peppermint.

icing — a special top layer, or frosting, used on a cake or other baked goods.

ingredients — all the different substances, materials, or parts that make up a recipe or product.

mixture — a blend of two or more ingredients.

party — a group of people who get together to have fun or to celebrate a special event.

recipe — the specific instructions to follow when cooking or baking. A recipe lists exactly which ingredients you need, how much of each ingredient you need, how to mix the ingredients properly, and how long and at what temperature to bake or cook them.

whip — to beat with a spoon, beater, or whisk.

Places to Visit

Everything we do involves some basic scientific principles. Listed below are a few museums that offer a variety of scientific information and experiences. You may also be able to locate other museums in your area. Just remember: you don't always have to visit a museum to experience the wonders of science. Science is everywhere!

Hershey Museum
170 South Hersheypark Drive
Hershey, PA 17033

The Smithsonian Institution
1000 Jefferson Drive SW
Washington, D.C. 20560

Ontario Science Center
770 Don Mills Road
Don Mills, Ontario
M3C 1T3

Royal British Columbia Museum
675 Belleville Street
Victoria, British Columbia
V8V 1X4

Field Museum of Natural History
Roosevelt Road at
    Lake Shore Drive
Chicago, IL 60605

More Books to Read

The Bake-A-Cake Book
    Marie Meyer
    (Chronicle)

The Children's Step-by-Step Cookbook
    A. Wilkes (Dorling Kindersley)

Cooking Wizardry for Kids
  Margaret Kenda
  (Childrens Press)

My First Baking Book
  Helen Drew
  (Knopf)

How to Make an Apple Pie and
  See the World
  Marjorie Priceman (Knopf)

My First Cookbook
  Angela Wilkes
  (Dorling Kindersley)

Videotapes

Kids in the Kitchen
  (Imagination Tree)

My First Cooking Video
  (Sony)

Index